ESSENTIAL SONGS FOR

cello

Available for
FLUTE, CLARINET, ALTO SAX, TENOR SAX, TRUMPET,
HORN, TROMBONE, VIOLIN, VIOLA, CELLO

ISBN 978-1-4234-5540-0

HAL•LEONARD®

Visit Hal Leonard Online at
www.halleonard.com

Contact Us:
Hal Leonard
7777 West Bluemound Road
Milwaukee, WI 53213
Email: info@halleonard.com

In Europe contact:
Hal Leonard Europe Limited
42 Wigmore Street
Marylebone, London, W1U 2RN
Email: info@halleonardeurope.com

In Australia contact:
Hal Leonard Australia Pty. Ltd.
4 Lentara Court
Cheltenham, Victoria, 3192 Australia
Email: info@halleonard.com.au

CONTENTS

ALL SHOOK UP

CELLO

Words and Music by OTIS BLACKWELL
and ELVIS PRESLEY

ALL THE WAY

from THE JOKER IS WILD

CELLO

Words by SAMMY CAHN
Music by JAMES VEN HEUSEN

AND I LOVE HER

CELLO

Words and Music by JOHN LENNON
and PAUL McCARTNEY

ANYONE CAN WHISTLE
from ANYONE CAN WHISTLE

CELLO

Words and Music by
STEPHEN SONDHEIM

Slowly and tenderly

AUTUMN LEAVES

CELLO

English lyrics by JOHNNY MERCER
French lyrics by JACQUES PREVERT
Music by JOSEPH KOSMA

BABY, I LOVE YOUR WAY

Words and Music by
PETER FRAMPTON

CELLO

BACK AT ONE

CELLO

Words and Music by
BRIAN McKNIGHT

BEAUTIFUL

CELLO

Words and Music by
LINDA PERRY

BECAUSE OF YOU

CELLO

Words and Music by KELLY CLARKSON,
DAVID HODGES and BEN MOODY

Moderately

BENNIE AND THE JETS

CELLO

Words and Music by ELTON JOHN
and BERNIE TAUPIN

BLESS THE BROKEN ROAD

CELLO

Words and Music by MARCUS HUMMON,
BOBBY BOYD and JEFF HANNA

D.S. al Coda

CODA

BORN FREE

from the Columbia Pictures' Release BORN FREE

CELLO

Words by DON BLACK
Music by JOHN BARRY

BRING HIM HOME
from LES MISÉRABLES

Music by CLAUDE-MICHEL SCHÖNBERG
Lyrics by HERBERT KRETZMER and ALAIN BOUBLIL

Cello

BREATHE

CELLO

Words and Music by HOLLY LAMAR
and STEPHANIE BENTLEY

Moderately fast

BYE BYE LOVE

CELLO

Words and Music by FELICE BRYANT
and BOUDLEAUX BRYANT

CALIFORNIA GIRLS

CELLO

Words and Music by BRIAN WILSON
and MIKE LOVE

Moderate Shuffle Rock

CAN YOU FEEL THE LOVE TONIGHT

from Walt Disney Pictures' THE LION KING

CELLO

Music by ELTON JOHN
Lyrics by TIM RICE

Pop Ballad

THE CHICKEN DANCE

CELLO

By TERRY RENDALL
and WERNER THOMAS

CLIMB EV'RY MOUNTAIN
from THE SOUND OF MUSIC

CELLO

Lyrics by OSCAR HAMMERSTEIN II
Music by RICHARD RODGERS

Majestically

CRAZY LITTLE THING CALLED LOVE

CELLO

Words and Music by
FREDDIE MERCURY

COMPLICATED

CELLO

Words and Music by AVRIL LAVIGNE,
LAUREN CHRISTY, SCOTT SPOCK
and GRAHAM EDWARDS

Moderate Pop

CROCODILE ROCK

CELLO

Words and Music by ELTON JOHN
and BERNIE TAUPIN

DANCING QUEEN

CELLO

Words and Music by BENNY ANDERSSON,
BJORN ULVAEUS and STIG ANDERSON

Strong Rock

DON'T KNOW WHY

CELLO

Words and Music by
JESSE HARRIS

DREAM LOVER

CELLO

Words and Music by
BOBBY DARIN

DROPS OF JUPITER
(Tell Me)

Cello

Words and Music by PAT MONAHAN,
JIMMY STAFFORD, ROB HOTCHKISS,
CHARLIE COLIN and SCOTT UNDERWOOD

DUST IN THE WIND

CELLO

Words and Music by
KERRY LIVGREN

EASTER PARADE

from AS THOUSANDS CHEER

CELLO

Words and Music by
IRVING BERLIN

ENDLESS LOVE

CELLO

Words and Music by
LIONEL RICHIE

FEVER

CELLO

Words and Music by JOHN DAVENPORT
and EDDIE COOLEY

FIRE AND RAIN

CELLO

Words and Music by
JAMES TAYLOR

THE FIRST CUT IS THE DEEPEST

CELLO

Words and Music by
CAT STEVENS

THE FOOL ON THE HILL

CELLO

Words and Music by JOHN LENNON
and PAUL McCARTNEY

Slowly

FOOTLOOSE

Theme from the Paramount Motion Picture FOOTLOOSE

Cello

Words by DEAN PITCHFORD
and KENNY LOGGINS
Music by KENNY LOGGINS

FROM A DISTANCE

CELLO

Words and Music by
JULIE GOLD

GO AWAY, LITTLE GIRL

CELLO

Words and Music by GERRY GOFFIN
and CAROLE KING

GOOD VIBRATIONS

CELLO

Words and Music by BRIAN WILSON
and MIKE LOVE

GOT MY MIND SET ON YOU

CELLO

Words and Music by
RUDY CLARK

A GROOVY KIND OF LOVE

CELLO

Words and Music by TONI WINE
and CAROLE BAYER SAGER

Moderately slow

HAPPY TOGETHER

CELLO

Words and Music by GARRY BONNER
and ALAN GORDON

HAPPY TRAILS

from the Television Series THE ROY ROGERS SHOW

CELLO

Words and Music by
DALE EVANS

HEAVEN

CELLO

Words and Music by BRYAN ADAMS
and JIM VALLANCE

HEAVEN

CELLO

Words and Music by HENRY GARZA,
JOEY GARZA and RINGO GARZA

HELLO

CELLO

Words and Music by
LIONEL RICHIE

HIGH HOPES

CELLO

Words by SAMMY CAHN
Music by JAMES VAN HEUSEN

HOW CAN YOU MEND A BROKEN HEART

CELLO

Words and Music by BARRY GIBB
and ROBIN GIBB

Slow beat

HOW SWEET IT IS (TO BE LOVED BY YOU)

CELLO

Words and Music by EDWARD HOLLAND,
LAMONT DOZIER and BRIAN HOLLAND

I GOT YOU
(I Feel Good)

CELLO

Words and Music by
JAMES BROWN

(Spoken:) Hey!

I HOPE YOU DANCE

CELLO

Words and Music by TIA SILLERS
and MARK D. SANDERS

I JUST CALLED TO SAY I LOVE YOU

CELLO

Words and Music by
STEVIE WONDER

Moderately

I LEFT MY HEART IN SAN FRANCISCO

CELLO

Words by DOUGLASS CROSS
Music by GEORGE CORY

I SHOT THE SHERIFF

CELLO

Words and Music by
BOB MARLEY

I WANT TO HOLD YOUR HAND

CELLO

Words and Music by JOHN LENNON
PAUL McCARTNEY

I'LL BE THERE

CELLO

Words and Music by BERRY GORDY,
HAL DAVIS, WILLIE HUTCH
and BOB WEST

I'LL BE

CELLO

Words and Music by
EDWIN McCAIN

I'M WITH YOU

Cello

Words and Music by AVRIL LAVIGNE, LAUREN CHRISTY,
SCOTT SPOCK and GRAHAM EDWARDS

Moderately

IF

CELLO

Words and Music by
DAVID GATES

IF I HAD A HAMMER

(The Hammer Song)

CELLO

Words and Music by LEE HAYS
and PETE SEEGER

THE IMPRESSION THAT I GET

CELLO

Words and Music by DICKY BARRETT
and JOE GITTLEMAN

IN THE MOOD

CELLO

By JOE GARLAND

IT'S A SMALL WORLD

from "it's a small world" at Disneyland Park and Magic Kingdom Park

CELLO

Words and Music by RICHARD M. SHERMAN
and ROBERT B. SHERMAN

IT'S TOO LATE

CELLO

Words and Music by CAROLE KING
and TONI STERN

ITSY BITSY TEENIE WEENIE
YELLOW POLKADOT BIKINI

CELLO

Words and Music by PAUL VANCE
and LEE POCKRISS

Moderately

THEME FROM "JURASSIC PARK"

from the Universal Motion Picture JURASSIC PARK

CELLO

Composed by
JOHN WILLIAMS

KING OF THE ROAD

CELLO

Words and Music by
ROGER MILLER

LA BAMBA

CELLO

By RITCHIE VALENS

LET IT BE

CELLO

Words and Music by JOHN LENNON
PAUL McCARTNEY

LISTEN TO WHAT THE MAN SAID

CELLO

Words and Music by
PAUL and LINDA McCARTNEY

THE LOCO-MOTION

CELLO

Words and Music by GERRY GOFFIN
and CAROLE KING

LOUIE, LOUIE

CELLO

Words and Music by
RICHARD BERRY

LOVE ME TENDER

CELLO

Words and Music by ELVIS PRESLEY
and VERA MATSON

Moderately slow

LUCY IN THE SKY WITH DIAMONDS

CELLO

Words and Music by JOHN LENNON
and PAUL McCARTNEY

MAMBO NO. 5
(A Little Bit Of...)

CELLO

Original Music by DAMASO PEREZ PRADO
Words by LOU BEGA and ZIPPY

ME AND BOBBY McGEE

CELLO

Words and Music by KRIS KRISTOFFERSON
and FRED FOSTER

A MOMENT LIKE THIS

CELLO

Words and Music by JOHN REID
and JORGEN KJELL ELOFSSON

MY FAVORITE THINGS

from THE SOUND OF MUSIC

CELLO

Lyrics by OSCAR HAMMERSTEIN II
Music by RICHARD RODGERS

Lively, with spirit

THE ODD COUPLE

Theme from the Paramount Picture THE ODD COUPLE
Theme from the Paramount Television Series THE ODD COUPLE

CELLO

By NEAL HEFTI

ON TOP OF SPAGHETTI

CELLO

Words and Music by
TOM GLAZER

Moderately fast, with spirit

100 YEARS

CELLO

Words and Music by
JOHN ONDRASIK

ONE NOTE SAMBA
(Samba de uma nota so)

CELLO

Original Lyrics by NEWTON MENDONCA
English Lyrics by ANTONIO CARLOS JOBIM
Music by ANTONIO CARLOS JOBIM

PETER COTTONTAIL

CELLO

Words and Music by STEVE NELSON
and JACK ROLLINS

PUPPY LOVE

CELLO

Words and Music by
PAUL ANKA

Moderately slow

QUE SERA, SERA
(Whatever Will Be, Will Be)
from THE MAN WHO KNEW TOO MUCH

Words and Music by JAY LIVINGSTON
and RAY EVANS

CELLO

Moderately bright

R.O.C.K. IN THE U.S.A
(A Salute to 60's Rock)

CELLO

Words and Music by
JOHN MELLENCAMP

THE RAINBOW CONNECTION
from THE MUPPET MOVIE

CELLO

Words and Music by PAUL WILLIAMS
and KENNETH L. ASCHER

RAINDROPS KEEP FALLIN' ON MY HEAD
from BUTCH CASSIDY AND THE SUNDANCE KID

CELLO

Lyric by HAL DAVID
Music by BURT BACHARACH

ROCKIN' ROBIN

CELLO

Words and Music by
J. THOMAS

SAILING

CELLO

Words and Music by
CHRISTOPHER CROSS

SEE YOU LATER, ALLIGATOR

CELLO

Words and Music by
ROBERT GUIDRY

SEVENTY SIX TROMBONES
from Meredith Willson's THE MUSIC MAN

CELLO

By MEREDITH WILLSON

March tempo

SHAKE, RATTLE AND ROLL

CELLO

Words and Music by
CHARLES CALHOUN

SHOUT

CELLO

Words and Music by ROLAND ORZABAL
and IAN STANLEY

SIXTEEN GOING ON SEVENTEEN
from THE SOUND OF MUSIC

CELLO

Lyrics by OSCAR HAMMERSTEIN II
Music by RICHARD RODGERS

SMOOTH

CELLO

Words by ROB THOMAS
Music by ROB THOMAS and ITALL SHUR

Medium Latin Rock

SO NICE
(Summer Samba)

CELLO

Original Words and Music by MARCOS VALLE
and PAULO SERGIO VALLE
English Words by NORMAN GIMBEL

Moderately

THE SOUND OF MUSIC

from THE SOUND OF MUSIC

CELLO

Lyrics by OSCAR HAMMERSTEIN II
Music by RICHARD RODGERS

SPINNING WHEEL

CELLO

Words and Music by
DAVID CLAYTON THOMAS

SPLISH SPLASH

CELLO

Words and Music by BOBBY DARIN
and MURRAY KAUFMAN

With a beat

STAND BY ME

CELLO

Words and Music by JERRY LEIBER,
MIKE STOLLER and BEN E. KING

SUNNY

CELLO

Words and Music by
BOBBY HEBB

Moderate Rock

SUPERCALIFRAGILISTICEXPIALIDOCIOUS

from Walt Disney's MARY POPPINS

CELLO

Words and Music by RICHARD M. SHERMAN
and ROBERT B. SHERMAN

Brightly

SURFIN' U.S.A.

CELLO

Words and Music by
CHUCK BERRY

TAKIN' CARE OF BUSINESS

CELLO

Words and Music by
RANDY BACHMAN

Moderate Rock

TEARS IN HEAVEN

CELLO

Words and Music by ERIC CLAPTON
and WILL JENNINGS

TENNESSEE WALTZ

CELLO

Words and Music by REDD STEWART
and PEE WEE KING

Easy Waltz

THAT'LL BE THE DAY

Cello

Words and Music by JERRY ALLISON,
NORMAN PETTY and BUDDY HOLLY

THIS LOVE

CELLO

Words and Music by ADAM LEVINE
and JESSE CARMICHAEL

TIE A YELLOW RIBBON
ROUND THE OLE OAK TREE

CELLO

Words and Music by L. RUSSELL BROWN
and IRWIN LEVINE

TIJUANA TAXI

CELLO

Words by JOHNNY FLAMINGO
Music by ERVAN "BUD" COLEMAN

Moderately

TRUE COLORS

CELLO

Words and Music by BILLY STEINBERG
and TOM KELLY

THE TWIST

CELLO

Words and Music by
HANK BALLARD

UP WHERE WE BELONG

from the Paramount Picture AN OFFICER AND A GENTLEMAN

CELLO

Words by WILL JENNINGS
Music by BUFFY SAINTE-MARIE and JACK NITZSCHE

WALKING IN MEMPHIS

CELLO

Words and Music by
MARC COHN

THE WAY YOU LOOK TONIGHT
from SWING TIME

Cello

Words by DOROTHY FIELDS
Music by JEROME KERN

WE ARE FAMILY

CELLO

Words and Music by NILE RODGERS
and BERNARD EDWARDS

WE ARE THE CHAMPIONS

CELLO

Words and Music by
FREDDIE MERCURY

WE BUILT THIS CITY

Cello

Words and Music by BERNIE TAUPIN, MARTIN PAGE,
DENNIS LAMBERT and PETER WOLF

WE'VE ONLY JUST BEGUN

CELLO

Words and Music by ROGER NICHOLS
and PAUL WILLIAMS

WHITE FLAG

CELLO

Words and Music by RICK NOWELS,
ROLLO ARMSTRONG and DIDO ARMSTRONG

A WHOLE NEW WORLD

from Walt Disney's ALADDIN

CELLO

Music by ALAN MENKEN
Lyrics by TIM RICE

Sweetly

Y.M.C.A.

CELLO

Words and Music by JACQUES MORALI,
HENRI BELOLO and VICTOR WILLIS

YESTERDAY

CELLO

Words and Music by JOHN LENNON
and PAUL McCARTNEY

Moderately, with expression

YOU ARE MY SUNSHINE

CELLO

Words and Music by
JIMMIE DAVIS

YOU LIGHT UP MY LIFE

CELLO

Words and Music by
JOSEPH BROOKS

YOU ARE THE MUSIC IN ME

from the Disney Channel Original Movie HIGH SCHOOL MUSICAL 2

CELLO

Words and Music by
JAMIE HOUSTON

139

YOU'RE BEAUTIFUL

CELLO

Words and Music by JAMES BLUNT,
SACHA SKARBEK and AMANDA GHOST

YOU'RE STILL THE ONE

Cello

Words and Music by SHANIA TWAIN
and ROBERT JOHN LANGE

YOU'VE GOT A FRIEND IN ME

from Walt Disney's TOY STORY

CELLO

Music and Lyrics by
RANDY NEWMAN

YOUR SONG

CELLO

Words and Music by ELTON JOHN
and BERNIE TAUPIN

ZOOT SUIT RIOT

CELLO

Words and Music by
STEVE PERRY

Spoken: Blow, dad-dy!